The Mellifluous Trills

An Anthology of Poems

Durbadal Ghibela

ISBN 978-93-5610-143-2
© Durbadal Ghibela 2022
Published in India 2022 by Pencil

A brand of
One Point Six Technologies Pvt. Ltd.
123, Building J2, Shram Seva Premises,
Wadala Truck Terminal, Wadala (E)
Mumbai 400037, Maharashtra, INDIA
E connect@thepencilapp.com
W www.thepencilapp.com

DISCLAIMER: *The opinions expressed in this book are those of the authors and do not purport to reflect the views of the Publisher.*

Author biography

Durbadal Ghibela is presently working as a Reader in English in Jarasingha HSS, Jarasingha in the District of Balangir in Odisha (India). He has tremendous passion for writing poems in English. He has the credit of being the co-author of a number of Anthology of Poems and this is his fourth Anthology as three Anthologies - Voice of Serenity, Shimmering Pearls and Resonance of Heart have already been published by Publishers of International repute.As an active member of National and International Poetry Forums he has acclaimed distinctive niche for his outstanding creativity.

CONTENTS

Epigraph

The Anthology 'The Mellifluous Trills' exposes the melodies of diverse emotions brimming with the essence of life.

Preface

Life is a prolonged journey combined with pain and pleasure, success and failure, cheer and remorse, glory and defeat and the like. And we the humans are mere travellers marching towards the destination. Everyone has the aim to reach the threshold of victory wading the path through the adversities. And some on the way are disheartened by failure but some other regain strength and courage regarding the hindrances as the essence of life. In fact , to accomplish a task there may be obstacles, hopelessness,disappointment but a wise man never bows head before all these negative forces. At such moments of bewilderment noble thoughts of the great souls act as a beacon light to show us the right path. Their ideals guide us to discard melancholy and frustration and proceed with valour and resolution. Further, the ideas and thoughts intertwined in the various forms of genres inspire the mind to be confident and fearless. In this regard the poems incorporated in the Anthology might boost up the enthusiasm of the readers and take the lead as the greater force of joy, cheer and encouragement.

Durbadal Ghibela

Acknowledgements

The moment I dribble my thought in the form of poems I feel behind it there lies the blessings of the Omniscient God, the creator of the Universe.So at the outset I cannot but bow my head before the Almighty for His bliss upon a mere human like me.

All the members of my family deserve high praise for their consistent help and support behind this great endeavour.

I tip my hat to the the whole team of PENCIL PUBLICATION for providing me a suitable platform and support for the publication of this Anthology.

Introduction

The Anthology 'The Mellifluous Trills' is an endeavour to present the multifarious thoughts comman in human life. The purpose of this enterprise will come out successful , if the loving readers come forward to revere the novelty behind the thoughts in the poems. Moreover, as a token of love, the Anthology might leave indelible marks in the minds of the enthusiastic readers.

Durbadal Ghibela

Essence of Life

Beginning from birth

to the last breath

Life is a blend of pain and pleasure

Equanimity affords ample strength

Grit and confidence are

the hidden treasure.

Life is empty but for noble deeds

And so synonymous with action

The brave hearts

always take the lead

But the cowards lose and atone.

Life is not merely a bed of roses

Rather the mingling of

joy hardship and toil

Many get entangled in life's mazes

Failing to calm down mind's turmoil.

Life is a long pilgrimage

to endow it with divine bliss

And disseminate the sublime message

Of fraternity, love and peace.

Soul of Poetry

The soul of poetry

Resonant with imagery

The sound it induces

Exults the memory.

The soothing note

Makes the cuckoo sing

Beckons the spring

Trees rustle in rapture

Rain dances with nature

The poet's breathing words

With mesmeric sound

Holds the creation spellbound.

Mother

The burden of the womb

Lightens after nine months of pain

Convulsion makes the body

numb for the new creation.

Never can the onlookers feel

Nor expressible is the tremor

It's only the mother's thrill

The baby unaware for ever.

The mother's inexplicable labour

Later merges in the severity of the son

His inhumanity makes her suffer

But she is as noble as earth and heaven.

Knot

The knot of anguish stiffening

Loosened by a great heart's compassion,

The knot of isolation from love

Unfastened by tender affection.

The knot of the capricious fate

Unhooked by valour and credence

The knot of distinction and glory undone

With divine bliss and credence.

Separation

Goodnight, goodnight !

Parting in such sweet sorrow,

that I shall say

goodnight till tomorrow.

Bidding adieu to moments of buoyancy

leaves me in irking sorrow

the mirth of utopia

sinks in endless throes.

Eyes can't bear

the spasm of separation

inundated in melancholic conundrum.

Still with shattered emotion

embrace the pang

and heart I show for

the jab of the venomous fang.

Force of Love

The resplendent property in man

left for others

the outcome of the paroxysm

and harbinger of trains of omen.

It forfeited Adam and Eve

of the bright paradise

following the tasting of fruit

from the forbidden tree.

Binds the mother and son

the hypnotic gift of the Omnipotent.

inflates and ebbs

which the lovers and beloveds feel.

Love !

Very powerful to sway the existence

but 'Eternal Love…'

expounds the path of

jolly and excellence.

The Poor Fellow

Shabby, disheveled

the forlorn being

spreading tattered cloth

in the temples' front

in the crowded fairs

on the foot paths

with the bag of yearning

amidst ire and mercy.

Stretching hands

trying to please

the passers-by

with the usual words.

Some have a kind heart

throwing a small coin

some leaving uncaring

and some frowning.

The poor fellow

knows the mass

and goes

with the same routine

not having

contempt and rage

like the passers-by.

Envy

The dreaded enemy

Destroys purity and joviality

Foils mind with hatred

Rocks the wit

Kills the spirit

Traps one in the snare.

And the victim

In the grip of envy

Gets strangulated

And finds no difference

Between amity and enmity

And the harrowing effect

Ruins the entity.

On the Bridge

The sweet murmur

of the snaky river

the view all around

keeps me still

on the bridge.

Trees dancing

in the lyre

of the wind.

Birds in the sporting

with luxury

like a new born babe

the sun sprinkles

the golden light.

The horizon

adds to the decoration

adorable

the store of her palace

and on the

cool moment

of a fine morning

the scenic beauty

washes gloominess

meditating

for a while

on the bridge.

Her Nobility

No one to excel her

for the breast oozes

a perfuming juice

sweetening, ennobling

the peeping, dancing

the blest growth.

Heart with loving care

selfless prayer

enduring pangs

and still unshaken

anchoring

the blissful child.

The magnanimous soul

swells for the budding plant

and in some painful moments

the growth

laughs at her

frets and fumes

burns her sensation

and she has a noble heart

and every moment

has a keen eye

on the blessed creation

till her death.

Light in Darkness

Dwelling in darkness

no trait of modernity

not close to splendour

but have a lot

noble and extolling.

Beauty in its bud

pleasure unblossomed

knowledge confined

for a long way

from the bustle of life.

Pure and stainless hearts

receiving with affability

strangers to them known

all in good time.

Here is left

Gandhi's non-violence

Christ's brotherhood

here is the home of God

here is the sound

of the holy scriptures

here is the glorification

and light in darkness.

The Fanciful Lover

The fanciful lad

stirred the still water

throwing pebbles

never expecting

the unending ripples.

Now counting circles

the whole day

killing precious moments

moving his eye

from the centre

to the unimagined.

roving and roving

for the damsel of dream

who has moved his heart

and still obstinate

to make the water still.

Life in Reality

From the tempestuous sea

the life ship to be taken ashore

gaining the wealth of peace and happiness

with the rudder of courage and confidence.

The fruit to be tasted

with great relish

lighting the darkness of sorrow and decadence.

The thorns to be treaded

taking refuge on the lap of

tolerance and patience.

The goal to be reached

struggling and struggling

as life's essence.

The blessed life to be heightened

showering the light of love

discarding envy, rage and violence.

The mind to be enlightened

to be emboldened,to be ennobled

with an invocation to the Omniscient

and with beacon light and divine grace.

In her Sadness

Comes the monster

to rob of to crumple

her possession.

The saree loses colour

the hands forget the jingling

disappears the vermillion

eyes fear to anoint collyrium

become teary

disappears the lac-dye

body quivers in its entirety.

And lo !

She deserves

a heart rending word

for her lord,for her destitution.

Her family boat rocking

but she is at pains

rowing with the oar of patience

to march ahead balancing

her tottering legs

and consoling

the bereaved heart

in her sadness.

The Memory

On the fateful day of August thirteen

Of the year two thousand nineteen.

Long hours of awful torrential rain

Rocked and afflicted people's brains.

Record rain fall of 555 millimetre

Apprehensions made many a heart flutter.

They gazed at the clouds in wonder

To know if there was any fissure.

Rain flooded on roads,lanes and gutters

Marooned in houses some craved for succour.

Houses at low levels submerged in water

People climbed the roof tops out of fear.

The gush of water was swift and terrible

Battered the houses, roads and bridges to crumble.

Boats rescued those in great distress

Victims in neck deep water prayed the Almighty to bless.

Thank God ! rain receded before the evening

Partially slackened the inexpressible suffering.

The mayhem ripped the hearts with damage and loss

The reminiscence of the day bewilders mind with throbs.

Curiosity

Curiosity is curiously woven

in the curious web of life

its horrible touch opens

terrible fatal cavern

but her gentle kiss

shows the height of perfection

novelty and innovation

sphere of enlightenment

aroma of elevation

and unthinkable amelioration.

Fear

In the grip of fear

we turn cowards

toning down bravery

confidence collides with instability

feet totter in anxiety.

In the clutch of fear

we feel in heart

a great tremor

we reel back often for

reasons unknown

because we have fear

as the crown.

Moonlight

The bleakness

set my pensive mood alight

I woke up

from my bed outright.

Came out to rejoice

the moon light at midnight

The luscious illumination

wrecked my fright.

The moon descended

to my fancy

And whispered

her words of ecstasy

Anger

Befooled by

the tides of emotion

you are in the grip of

razing anger.

The venom sprawls

 in the nerves

vanquishing your

joy and cheer.

You feel you clamp down

someone with your anger

but the truth is

you are subjugated

 by its unshakeable power.

Rain Queen

From behind the panoramic show

Accompanied by the cooling breeze

Clouds in their wondrous frolic

Foliage nodding to join the music

Lightning welcoming the start anew

Rain Queen with the heart of rejoice

Descends from palanquin fanciful

To stun the earth with allaying grace

Dance the creatures in ample glee

Beholding Rain Queen in chivalrous spree.

The Voyage

The endless journey

stretching from

land to sea

earth to heaven

light to darkness

sometimes straight

sometimes curvy.

The life ship struggling

to touch the destiny

exceeding the tempest

with the rudder of

patience and confidence.

Violent jolts rocking

the joyous moments

but still

the ship voyaging

to smell

the odour of

hopes and yearnings.

An Agonizing Moment

Only my presence

In the lonely compartment

Intolerable and envied

By the lovelorn couple.

The infuriated eyes

Burning with anger

For the freedom

Was marred.

Mind was crushed

Between the pensive mood of

To be or not to be.

Nothingness put me to shame

And pretended

Enjoying the outer view

Through the window

Prayed not to be crushed

By the pure bond

And swallowing evil thoughts

Till coming to the destination.

She Knows not

She knows not

the definition of Shakespeare.

"Love is not love

which alters when it alteration finds."

She knows not

the Ravan in disguise

spreading the snare of illusion

to afflict her alive.

She knows not the truth-

once she is in hell

she will be dead alike.

She knows not the water

that leaves the fish in the net

though companion in last life.

She knows not the man

claiming the source of life

but in reality a liar and a cheat.

The Dancer

The bulging body

and playful eyes

pulls me

to call her a dancer.

she may not be

or may be unaware

of the art

and still

I will call her a dancer

for her face moves

eyes dance

and dances

the body and heart

and for my eyes

perceive her dance

like a dancer.

Dream

Dream and reality poles apart

and dreaming of regal splendor

traversing in the air on horse back

the stunned beauty

the heavenly pleasure merges

in the morning hubbub

in the regained consciousness

and it leaves no pangs

no repentation,no atonement.

But when the conscious mind's

dream of making home a heaven

deep rooted fidelity

and long cherished hopes

disappear in mid air

may be for it is destined

or as vicissitudes

and this violent jolt explodes

the dancing heart.

Then life feels

dream is dream

and reality only gleams

sometimes in the dream.

For the Motherland

Near and dear ones afar

family affection chained

choking in between

longing and commitment

stirred by dreamy past

living present,glorious future

but heartened by unyielding guts

only for the mother land.

The youthful joy left behind

solitary moments

piercing the heart

with wife's glimmering face

her endearing smile

her solacing words.

Sighing for home

remembering the rapturous faces

and soothing voices of the lovely kids

and still tolerant and patient

shouldering the noble responsibility

shadowing the delightful distance

only for the mother land.

The menace of Kargil war

devastation of terrorism

threat of aggression

keeping the vigilant heroes

dauntless, determined

And on maneuvers

indomitable courage

only for the mother land.

The pride of the nation

the daring saviours

marching ahead

 with great devotion

and a spirit of sacrifice

only for the mother land.

Youth

Youth passes at a snail's pace

leaving behind the churned past.

Anxiety smashes the present

Turning the pages of the last.

Mind deeps into the unwanted

Whirling and whirling in the earth.

Body assimilates the pain

Hoping for the new birth.

Heart accelerates the beat

Reminding the dubious role.

Senses go out of control

Thinking always of the whole.

Life drinks sorrows and tears

Closing the eyes of tolerance

Everything pricks body and mind

And still admitting defeat

To taste it with patience.

Eclipse

In the space of the mind

the gravitational force of

Divine power

holds the heavenly body of

mortality

and the revolutionary transition

caressed by

the monstrous ray of lunacy

sometimes eclipses

the moon of celestial glee

when only

the darkness of our follies

we can see.

Mourn not

Mourn not feeling my soul out of body

I am not so.

The body is not numb.

I am millions of stars that shine

Moving in deep sea I am on cloud nine

I am the morning sun of scathing winter

I am the lulling summer shower

Amidst the souls asleep and silent

I am the voice sweet and sonorant

Of the storm fiery and turbulent

I am the serene sky inspiring and vibrant

Do not lose your heart or lament

I am still breathing and potent.

Enough for Us

Mourn not as the sole loser

Failure will open the right threshold

Weep not for the heart is broken

Or else woes are manifold

In abject penury you can find

People shimmering in elation

Adversities synonymous with struggle

Precious jewel is our determination

Dearth of possession not the concern

In the still mind will happiness bloom

One blest with riches

Tomorrow may meet the doom

Life,wealth and youth transitory

Boast not of on the trivial

No one can undermine your place

Till you are resolute,confident and convivial

Human life is of great worth

When explored light in darkness

With mountainous heart and zeal

One can conquer ego and meanness

The world has enough for us

Strength of mind is the affluence

With magnanimity and benevolence

Let us diffuse our entrancing fragrance

Dissolution of Humanity

Day by day humanity biting the dust

Conscience under the yoke of lust

For a woman mind corrupt and unjust

Shamefully brutes have lecherous gust

As the victim of emotional burst

She is in ignominy and melancholy lost.

Who will call them civilised or educated ?

When their intuition is frozen and dead

Embossing in heart feelings unshed

Even if character or dignity assassinated

Her tenderness like a marionette toyed

Is she born only to be enjoyed ?

Frail and dumb for their ravenous appetite

Secured not at night or at broad daylight

Draws their mercy after in plight

Nothing will compensate the agony and spite

Unless she is revered with humane insight

Manhood would always deserve

disgrace,malice and slight.

The Enthralling Fragrance

Born with the same blood

Thoughts and actions different

Creations of the same Almighty

Beliefs and inclinations divergent

Worthless pride of caste and community

Unaware of cordial relation

Excited to ignite communal riot

An insignia of social disintegration

Violence begets brutality and blood shed

Love and amity showers divinity

Communal feuds limit to hatred

Brotherhood garners peace and charity

Fight for mere caste or community

Beyond the human cheer

Thinking the world a family

Beginning of prosperity and splendour

Let the light of peace glow for good

For amiable and amicable existence

Magnanimity of every human heart

Might disseminate the enthralling fragrance.

But for Future

For an optimist future is the hope to dream

There actions moving and candid

pop up to gleam

But for future the present empty and dark

Awaiting joy and cheer glistens like a spark

Vision of future infuses in us endless zeal

Enthusiasm fancied with good spirit

strengthens the will

Future segregated onset of abrupt end

Days ahead force behind the desire to intend

Present and future both sides of the same coin

Obliteration of future makes life rusted and barren.

Ambition

Immeasurable is the height of ambition

Unfathomable depth it carries on

Serene as the enchanting heaven

Massive sphere like that of the ocean

The force of the living desire

Nothing can vanquish or tire

The will of kissing the height

Magic behind the glory or might

Where ambition is the shield of life

One is the winner in the strife.

Actions

Actions small or big

unfathomable as the sea

high as the heaven

enormous as the universe

unimaginable as the mystery

of the Omnipotent God

cooling as the summer shower

amazing as the magic power

tender as the petals of a flower

sweet as honey, good as nectar

for they leave imprints indelible

bring great change in life

changes the course of the fate

may be like a drop of water

but moves like a spate.

Worthiness of Life

Life will be worthy

with noble actions

to march ,to toil

to challenge,to resist,to stand

to shine even after failure

to like even the betrayer

to help,to sympathise

to encourage,to embrace

to clad with humanity

to share,to ignite,to delight

to seek the grace of the Almighty

to shower affection

copious and limitless

to take the lead

to reach the destination

with valour and prowess.

Fountain of Love

The mounting flame of love

Scorching the ardour in me

Douses the fire with copious passion.

Look of your raving eyes

When digging furrows in my heart

Fill it with your fervent emotion.

The charm of your tender touches

Floating as the mist

Pour out your heartfelt elation.

Throw not me to

Dungeon of revulsion

Embrace me to quench the thirst.

Close not the threshold

Of your heart so amorous

Let me not be frigid frost.

Dry not ever the fountain of love

Let it run with eternal glow

Our love is not a bubble of water

To burst and end in wail and sorrow.

Rose

Variegated colours of rose in sight

Mind soaring with heavenly delight

Beauty scaling the unreachable height

Insignia of bond serene as night

Aromatic bloom to decor the might.

Reminds the love of my sweetheart

When love had its initial start

It is not a mere flower to behold

But the memory of pleasure untold

The floret in its numerous hues

Feelings tender and soothing brews.

The petals sweet and enchanting

Symbol of my love fresh and alluring.

Silhouette

In my drowsiness at midnight

in my secluded room

I gaze at my silhouette

on the wall in wonder

In the nucleus of the shadow

I hear the razing boom

Before defeating

my egotism in the battle

I fall into deep slumber.

Still in the dream

haunted by the silhouette

strangulating my arrogance

and whispering again and again

to stick to human essence.

A Poet's Thoughts

Gust of wind

not the harbinger of cyclone.

Blend of words

never adorns the writer's tone.

A few drops of water

not the vast ocean,

fusing mere words

cannot enliven a writer's pen.

Jumble of words

not the voice of music

but they can screech,

spontaneity of thoughts and emotions

radiant in appealing words

takes the writer

to the artistic niche.

Meet Me

The severity of your heart

rips me to pieces

Still your infidelity in me I suppress.

My love is immortal

you can never overlook

Dear Sweetheart !

You are my ever flowing brook.

Would you retreat with your soothing balm ?

For the lost love

if you are disgusted and weary

Meet me in the middle of your story.

When the soul is worn but wise

Pour out your emotion

with a different guise.

My love will never cease

and so imperishable

In your heart I am always there

And I will ever dribble.

If I have

If I hava

a superhero's superpower

I would bless all

with magnificent shower.

Magic potion

the humans will be given

To turn the world into a heaven.

Affinity and divinity

will prevail everywhere

Only peace and happiness

everyone will be aware.

Childhood Joy

Childhood glitter of

pranks and prattle,

babble and chuckle

Pinch and trickle,

yell and quarrel,

grin and cuddle

Words they fumble,

things they jumble,

cry and giggle

 A childish joy scatters

the noodle clothes in shamble

stares and goggles.

Prayer

In the new month

of the gay monsoon

I pray the Almighty

not to annihilate

the cheery mankind

with deluge and thunder.

I invoke the Omnipotent

to wipe away in the torrent

the misdemeanours

of the fragile hearts

and imbue in them with

sensibility and splendour.

A Poet and a Critic

The poet fancies the sky

to be wonderful and bright

The critic's mind wriggles

measuring its height.

A flower is enchanting

in the eyes of a poet

The critic bereft of emotion

thinks it a mere floret

The poet's heart dances

at the sight of rain

In it the critic perceives

the deluge and pain.

For a poet

the critic's mind is creative

For a critic

the poet's mind is delusive.

The Haunted House

Like the mystery of Bermuda Triangle

Or the Bhangarh Fort in eerie rumble

The haunted house is in ghostly tangle.

Those who know its harrowing conundrum

Never dare to come near the bedlam.

Sometimes the terrible howl of a wolf

Reverberates from down to the top roof.

The giggle and sobbing of the spirits

Even to a brave heart scares and afflicts.

The daredevils enter the house to know its secret

The next moment they scream and die in the garret.

Many have lost their lives with the place infatuated

The haunted house is still aloof and deserted.

The haunted house may have a real story

Or it may be hearsay ,hallucinatory or illusory

Do not be foolish to rush into something blurry.

Glow of Love

The unruly passion of love

overwhelmed with jubilation

leapt into the flame of sensation

glowed in the fire of predilection

battered the family relation

shattered social reputation

and proved herself blind

ocean of sorrow in mind

Cupid's heart so kind

it all started with tears

anchored in the heart

overflowed with cheers.

Magic

Salubrious weather

pervading all around

Immense joy made

my heart bound

I waved the magic wand anon

and chanted

the voodoo incantation.

The fairy of my dream

popped out in dazzle

Love in me began to sizzle.

My revelry basked

in the magic potion

The earthly worries

sank in the wizardry lotion.

Love and Lust

Love is the desire to share emotion

Lust is the carnal inundation.

The path of love runs to sanctity

Lust is the other name of insanity.

The purity of love God graces

Lust to satanic longings embraces.

Love uplifts heart to tranquility

Lust ends in hiatus and morbidity.

Love is calm,sweet,lasting and fragrant

Lust is frivolous,fiery,temporal and pungent.

Fake Smile

Tears of joy you cannot hide

the heart in pangs

your face will confide.

Black takes no other hue

like silver shines the sinew

you cannot suppress the disposition

malevolent and vile

the malignant intent peeps out

behind the fake smile.

Dearth versus Aspiration

Life is a desert

destination is barren

the long traverse

strewn with nothingness

life is vacuum

when there is

dearth of hopes and ambitions

dearth of desires and emotions.

The first step to

climb the ladder of success

rush into the citadel of glory

to clad in

the robe of aspirations.

Fantasy World

Roaming in the fantasy world

I am far from the vile

my unrealistic expectations

desist me from

ephemeral pleasure

for me not worthwhile.

My artistic mind can shower

joy solacing , everlasting

expectations of

plucking the twinkling stars

touching the ecstatic moon

fill me with enthusiasm

as to the ego and envy

of the real world

I do not cling.

Fancy

From the earth to heaven

From reality to wonderland

From idleness to nature

From melancholy to rapture

Fancy intertwined like the web

Of the toiling spider

As a shower of rain

Pouring on the emotion

Like the hum of the bees

Cooling the passion

Tidal waves of fancy

Roaring as the ocean

Peaceful visage with

Fragrant blooms woven

Recollected in tranquility

Luscious as nectar

Embracing in solitude

Steering as the Pole Star

Resort for the mind

Haunted by whirlwind of distress

Utopia to dispel

Fog of angst and helplessness.

Insanity

O heartless beings with feelings dry as stone !

Why do, the blade of notoriety, you hone ?

At broad daylight you ruin the modesty of women

For mere selfishness hearts with conspiracy woven

With your heinous crimes trembles the society

Innocent hearts victims of your insanity

In the claws of your cruelty and turbulence

Society has lost its essence

When the multitudes before your ill-will bow

Further, whose sleep will you steal now ?

You are not Forlorn

The world is not a deserted land

But the abode of gigantic hearts

In your moments of desperation

Cling not to remorse or wails

In your failure cry not

For you are not forlorn

At your loss or damage

Sit not fed up or dejected

Open your eyes and see

Who you were thinking your foes

One mocking at your helplessness

Those laughing at your penury

Assembled to pass their tender hands

On your heart on the verge of decay

Raise your head and see them

They have forgotten envy or ire

Aren't they your kith

Standing by your collapsing empire ?

Lost Moments

Moments of cheer and convulsion

Lost amidst the material maze

Sweet,alluring,spontaneous murmur

Died down to cautious whisper

Afraid of jeer and offence

Treading every step matching counts

Emotion hiding behind oozing passion

Gone are the days with soothing fervour

Hankering after money and pleasure

Hearts no less than hard stones

Life is blend of awe and shocking tones.

Tenacity

Darkness frightening as bleakness of hell
Enveloped by the gloom of doom
Murk of frail strain and dejection
Swallows the entity finding a room
Melancholy of loss or non-fulfillment
Suffocating as the dingy dungeon
Hopelessness and frustration in mere failure
Dreary as hard winter's domination
Will and spirit glowing as an eternal flame
Core of life and existence
Darkness is inevitable to feel the glimmer
Tenacity can fight the darkness of decadence.

Peace

Craving of every human

since time immemorial

The search pervading

to make life convivial

Some in the quest explore

strange places in confidence

Like the musk deer

looking all around for fragrance

In the stillness of the mind one can perceive

Coolness of the heart

the precious possession might contrive

Peace is not the artefact

to exchange for money

But the tranquility and contentment

with no tinge of agony

Blissful as the celestial light of eternity

Peace reigns where mind has

tolerance,composure and probity

Hesitate

Hesitate not to dribble

your compassion

when the humans are

in the claws of affliction.

The downtrodden in pangs

seek your mercy

hesitate not to

unfold the store of clemency.

All are humans

with the same blood

hesitate not to think them

noble creations of God.

Whisper

The whispers of the heart

resonates in the arid air

they root out the love

clung to the earth of emotions.

The posh garden of eternity

sneers at my nostalgia

earth underneath my feet

blush with endless tears

cry of solitude rips my cheer.

Noble whispers blowing as gale

shake my frozen love.

Inspiration

The inspiration of the loving wife

overjoys heart for a better life.

A friend's words of consolation

assuage remorse and desperation.

A teacher's words of essence

enlightens the path of existence.

Help of the near and dear in the society

adds to life spirit and joviality.

The light of grace of the Almighty

radiates contentment and prosperity.

My Country

Aroma of love in my country

binds people together.

Unity and integrity

peace and humanity

reign the nation

safeguarding her moral fervour.

The flag she unfurls

the ethics she adheres

pride and glory

and crown of splendour.

Circumstances

Circumstances reveal

honesty and integrity

as gold burning

validates its novelty.

Actions today or tomorrow

not the sum total of

real character.

The foot prints of

magnanimity we leave

on the sands of time

evince genuine nature.

Silence

Silence sometimes more fiery

than thunder and lightning

if not listened to

like an explosion

tears heart to smithereens

and joining them again

intensifies the silence

and the stillness of the soul

deafens the ears ,blinds the eyes

once more you lie

in the cavern of silence

to listen to its thrilling resonance.

If

Money and Wealth

Absolute hell

If devoid of

Peace and happiness.

What is the worth of

Gold and ivory

If the possession

Subverting the humaneness.

But a cottage

Furnished with

A string bed

And an old lantern

Better refuge

If here lies

The surge of fitness.

A sapphire

Or a mere flower

Precious for home and heart

If illuminated

With purity and excellence.

Son

An apple of the eye

flesh and blood of life

the soul of existence

light of the heart

wit of the mind

jewel of the head

the assembled emotion

the bowl of affection

for whom bleeds the heart

of the father

joy flows for ever

for whom the mother

pounds her bosom

for his elation

plunges into the cavern

the wreath of laurels

for the parents

glowing as the sun

the face of the loving son.

Loneliness

In a moment of loneliness

flows hot tears of remorse

the more I ponder

the more I stumble

the more I restrain

the more I fumble.

Jilted love in me

weeps and wails forever.

Shedding ocean of tears

mind is light as feather.

With the crushed heart

into the hell I am thrown

destiny is so cruel

for good I will repent and groan.

Fiction

Darkness is fuzzy

but it whispers

the eminence of light.

Scuffle with adversity

bitter and woeful

but its sweetness in the end

inspires and delight.

The face of sorrow

startling and petrifying

but the joy it garners

yodels an elegant trill.

The shadow of fiction

an amalgam of

truth in lie

and lie in truth

musing universal appeal.

You Can

The azure sky is a mere canopy

Its serendipity you have to explore

A flower has a captivating look

Invent its smile in store.

All the eyes behold the creation

But the perceptions differ.

The ears listen to varying sounds

The sonority and sweetness you prefer.

The world is a place of remorse

If you are a pessimist

You can spread here mirth and fragrance

If you are an optimist.

You see man as

An entity of flesh and blood

But the depth of your mind

Can reason him as a part of God.

Gaze at Me

The arrogance in you dear

crushes my longing and cheer.

Silence your words of magic

after you paralyse my life music.

The more you distance

the merrier your fragrance.

I pine for your enticing look

your smile is my ever flowing brook.

Your impressions engraved in my life

twangs the chords of my fife.

Do not unearth the seed of my love

fulfill its wondrous dream

but do not shove.

When you are haughty

my melancholies race

gaze at me

my joys will jump and dance.

Music in You

My dear !

you sound as a tambourine

From your smile

dribbles the music of violin.

So sweet is

your voice as a flute

The jingle of your words

accompany the mute.

You are my excitement

as the beating of the drum

In you vested

the varying tones

of the harmonium.

Movies

Materialism has engulfed

the modern man

Who cares the Titanic

or Pretty Woman

Those immersed in

painting,reading,writing

missing La La Land or

My Best Friend's Wedding

Watching a movie so long

many are disgusted

losing the charm of Titanic,

New Moon or Enchanted

The morals of many a movie

we do not endear

losing interest in Braveheart

Tangled or Gladiator.

Father

The backbone of a frail body

A crutch to meander.

The holy river of eternity

To quench the thirst for ever.

Epitome of inscribed emotions

Against the tender heart

Peeping out of affection

Clinging out of passion

Fondling out of exultation

Eyes with copious cheers

Overflowing the bowl of love.

An artist's blurred imagination

Beyond the poet's fancy

Reckon the estate

Father a lone word

Of limitless expressions

Heart full oblation.

Healthy Mind

Ailing body or mind

the yawning hiatus

the reverse extreme of

the east and the west

the earth and the heaven

predicament of

golden touch of king Midas.

But when sick body

is the derision of destiny

healthy-mind undeniable nectar

the wonderous potion

to assuage even the malignant soul.

You are so Loved

Very often when I recall

in me you bob up

the fountain of love in you

the ocean of mercy

the heaven of tranquility

shower of affability

the glitter of your face

the power of your grace

endless are your traits

that I cannot sum up.

Mother's Love

The succulent heart of mother

spring of the potion of

selfless love

unimaginable as the nectar

sweeter than luscious honey

bare as the earth

high as the sky

colossal as the ocean

calm as heaven

light as air

heavy as mountain

cool as the bower

fragrant as a flower

bright as light

angelic as sight

enchanting as the moon

enlightening as a boon

love of the magnanimous soul

mere words and phrases fail to extol.

Human values

People with riches

may be poor in rectitude

the haves-not may be in

uppish attitude

but mind clad with

human values

precious as diamond

powerful as uranium

bright as emerald

sways the multitudes.

Desolation

In the mist of desolation

my love is frozen and frosted

in the cream of my life

fatefully I am jilted.

Tedious is the traverse

the sole path bifurcated

battered and scattered emotion

makes me demented.

Though my paradise is lost

for the serpentine guile

my love is true and genuine

and my thoughts are agile.

A Moment in her Lap

Come out of the confined room for a while.

Come and behold the beautiful Nature

exposing her breast for everyone's rapture.

Come and beholdthe bewitching flowers

laughing like new-born babes

that can shower on you immense happiness.

Come and beholdthe rhythmic streams

moving with a tuneful sound

that can exult you by the forceful music.

Come and behold the full green trees

embracing in the bosoms the chirping birds

that can fill in you the delight

of the singing larks.

Come and behold her beautiful face

gleaming with the peeping of the sun

that can tranquilize your temperament

cleansing the agitation.

Come and sit only for a moment in her lap

to forget all your weariness

deserving her fondness.

Light of Life

Love is the light of life

to weed out the utter darkness of

spite and scorn.

the soothing ray

of the morning sun

to solace the hearts of millions.

Love is the fluroscent light of exuberance

to sparkle the glowing candle of affection.

Forfeiture of love rips humanity to shreds

and the sheer blackness is consumed

by the cavern inflaming with distress.

Poets are

Poets are the angels

uttering divine words of inspiration

beacon light reflecting the destination

full moon in life showering elation

fragrant flowers emanating

aroma of purification

nectar of life encompassing transition

generous souls leaving lasting impression

Store of ecstasy

sprinkling endless rejuvenation

generous hearts with excellence

uncommon minds with credence.

Mad in Love

Inundated in the sea of love

stuck to the cupid's arrow

lost in the world of elation

Shakuntala maddened by emotion

pining to merge in Dushmanta

yearning to shower the passion

craving for the sacred union

look of love in eyes

suppressed sounds of cries

restless like the whirlwind

convulsions endless in mind

unbearable Dushmanta's presence

throwing secret glance

pretending to remove the thorn

encompassing the lover's vision

overflows the river of desire

the sight of his enchanting face

oozes ocean of nectar.

Fire of Desire

The flames of desire razing

If not doused with restraint

The fire smears heart with ashes

When hot emotion gushes.

A plunge without prudence

Eats up heart bit by bit

And the crackling perplexes calmness

To fumble, tumble and crumble.

The heat empties life's essence

Filling the vacuum

with agony and repentance.

Magic Potion

Smile is the morning light

to warm the heart with elation

fragrant flower to spread

odour of harmony and correlation.

A piece of music to overwhelm

with trickle of affection

a drizzle to wash away

the filth of sorrow and affliction.

Smile is the wonderful magic potion

to diffuse the aroma of

geniality and cooperation.

Friendship

The blend of kindred hearts

sharing joy and compunction

The union of jubilant souls

seeking harmony and fusion.

The tie of amiable minds

imbued with mutual support

the strength of combined bosoms

standing ever in pleasant rapport.

Friendship is the divine bliss

adorned with faith and honesty

the shaft of seraphic light

stretching into the infinity

Apostle of Peace

The epitome of joviality and benevolence

apostle of peace and non violence.

Fusion of love and enlightenment

amalgam of kindness and contentment.

Spring of sacrifice and sanctity

Buddha- the soul of truth and probity.

Serenity is the great identity

Ideal of transformation is the entity.

Buddha is the embodiment of equality

with the ethos of universality.

Combating Corona

The rib of the world in quiver

for the threat of corona virus

with tremors of pandemic.

Relentless fight of multitudes

ending in tears and demise

with apprehensions and panic.

Antidote of social distancing

mask on mouth and nose

the weapons to fight the virus.

Cleaning hand with sanitiser

quarantine and containment

means to recuperate the loss.

In the moment of great crisis

awareness works wonders

but sociability turned dullish.

For good health and happiness

to combat the terrible virus

power of immunity we have to embellish.

The Unshaken Toiler

Imprints of blood and sweat

in the furrows of the hard soil

consistent endeavor, long wait

never disgusted with relentless toil.

The dream of reaping gold

with no care for winter or rain

capricious weather, vagaries manifold

striving hard in a stronger vein.

Bemoan the sons and the wife

for the stomach and clothing

luxury in the desolate life

a reverie and distant longing.

The harvest of the year

exhausts on the threshing floor

remains the land's muffled cheer

still unvanquished patience galore.

The Poor and the Rich

When one has a lot

they call him rich

and when lacks the bare necessities

poor in their eyes.

And those dreaming of skyscrapers every night

the thought of becoming a millionaire overnight

And beyond its reach.

The searchers of happiness all around

like the musk deer

looking for the perfume

the seekers of unexpected blessings

wealth from heaven and true happiness

in the beauties

in the maddening crowd

and finally entangled in the mirage.

And the assassinations of faith and humanity

the incarnation of devils

with the bags full of ill feeling

are really poor.

But those who feel the greatness

in small things

the wayfarers on the path of goodness

touching the destination

with the sweat of their brow

those devoid of sensual pleasure

the detached beings away from the lure of

earthly possessions.

The noble souls sacrificing the self

for the whole mankind

and the messiahs rescuing the world

from hollowness

have a lot in them and are truly rich.

Far From

Far from the din and bustle of life

Mind soars up under the tranquil sky

Passes over the frozen top of the Himalayas

Lured by the bliss of serenity

Rests in the hamlet calm and quiet

Unnoticed by malice and enmity

Beyond the reach of violence and inhumanity

Ego buried under the avalanche

Monotony swept away by icicles

Material joy of mundane world

Hibernating under the mounds of snow

Peace and happiness in spontaneity overflow

Heart dances in the chilling hamlet

Passion turning to a silhouette

Life rejoices the serendipity

Slumbering in the hamlet in placidity.

The Road not Taken

In the prolonged voyage of life

the roads to one's destination

many and varied.

Some studded with flowers

some with prick of thorns

great many a blend.

That uneven and blurred

with vile and guile

vitiated with treason and iniquity

lacerated with wildness and savagery

imbued with abomination and conceit

the road not taken

by those triumphant with

pageantry and distinction

composure and animation

beatitude and repletion.

When I need you

When I need you to quell my agony

You perch on my bosom in silence

And cleanse up all the sorrows

With your words sweet and sonorous

With your touch soft and amorous

When I need you in my solitude

You wipe off my monotony

I feel my life an utopia

Silence turns to an alluring song

In your jocund company.

When I need you to calm my passion

You are fragrant as a flower

The beauty of your tender petals

Mesmerize me with aroma of love

I bask in the enthralling shower.

When I need you to slumber in peace

In a while I doze

Listening to the lullaby you sing

You are my singing skylark

You are my eternal spring.

Came He

I gazed at the horizon

where the sky kissed the sea

my piercing look focussed

as far as they could

and implored the Almighty

to sweep away

the inflammation of the rueful heart

I visualised the ravishing force

out of the sea came He

stood cooling on the shore

his breath like the serene breeze

blew through my body

healing the smouldering sore.

www.ingramcontent.com/pod-product-compliance
Lightning Source LLC
LaVergne TN
LVHW050412160726
843469LV00041B/1047